Defining *the* Relationship

a relationship course for those considering marriage

DANNY SILK

LOVING ON PURPOSE
RELATIONSHIP SKILLS

www.lovingonpurpose.com

This manual has been designed
to be used in conjunction with the associated
DVD series Defining The Relationship

Second Edition © copyright 2011 Danny & Sheri Silk
www.LovingOnPurpose.com

Cover Graphics by Skyler Smith
Interior Design and Formatting by Lorraine Box
Developed and Edited by Laurie Freeman
Transcribed and Outlined by Stephanie Foster

ISBN # 978-0-9833895-0-7

This book is dedicated to all the people
who are living out covenant relationships
and are committed to showing this broken world
the healing power of love

We would like to personally thank

Earl & Darliene Johnson

Gene & Nell Nicolet

Bill & Beni Johnson

for showing Sheri and I the power
of generational blessing and inheritance

Our family has been transformed in one generation
because of your example of love and commitment

contents

Thank you for joining us as we lead you through this relationship course.

Most of what we know about relationships we learned from our own marriage. In 1984, Sheri and I entered a journey neither of us was ready for. It is difficult to be prepared for the unknown, but it was even more difficult for us to prepare for what was coming. Marriage would require both of us to completely change the way we had ever lived life, or for that matter, ever seen it lived. It took 15 years, Sheri says 12, of hanging on to our family while we were molded into totally different people. Many times it didn't look like we were going to make it. But thanks be to Jesus, through many tears, fights, and disconnects we forged a union that today, we will both die to protect.

Romance and the hope of being loved by someone are intoxicating. Many times, we unwittingly pull "God's will" into our desires to be with someone and end up plowing through the red flags as well as parental and leader input, which creates a situation God never intended. The term I use for this dynamic is *La La La.* It makes everything seem better than it really is and minimizes the issues that will destroy a relationship. *La La La* can walk you right into a poor decision.

Whether you are single, dating, or already engaged, this course will present you with perspective that only someone who has lived it can give. We hope to impart to you wisdom and understanding that empowers you both. The power that you will need comes from courage, the kind of courage that only truth can bring. When God speaks truth to our hearts, it ignites a courage that leads us to face our greatest fears.

Sometimes this fear is rejection and sometimes it's commitment. Either way, *Defining the Relationship* will allow you a rare opportunity to look that fear in the eye and make a grace-filled decision one way or the other. God bless you in this courageous adventure!

Danny & Sheri

Series
INTRODUCTION

1

Series INTRODUCTION

1

session one

CONTROL vs. FREEDOM
COURAGE
La La La **FACTOR**
CONNECTION
SERIES OUTLINE

instructor's goals

GIVE YOU INFORMATION
GIVE YOU UNDERSTANDING
GIVE YOU VALUE FOR PURPOSE
GIVE YOU COURAGE

CONTROL vs. FREEDOM

Control is a deadly element to every relationship.

- If you can understand who YOU are and who OTHERS are, you will come to the realization that being different isn't wrong.

- Learn to allow the person you are with to be who they are and learn to be yourself.

- If you can't be yourself and allow the person you are with to be themselves, being different will create anxiety for you.

- There are TWO people in every relationship.
  Mark 10:8 *"And the two shall become one flesh."*

"Now the Lord is the Spirit, and where the Spirit of the Lord is, there is freedom."
II Corinthians 3:17 (NIV)

**One of the experiences of love is
"you are *free* around me."**

- When we are in the presence of the Lord, we begin to change because we want to protect the love, freedom, and connection we have.

- Eventually, I get to be fully me and you get to be fully you.

- As we mature, the anxiety between us drops.

- The evidence of our love maturing is that I begin to manage myself differently in all my freedoms.

**When I refuse to manage myself to protect our love
or our connection, it is evidence,
"I don't understand, I am immature, and I am promoting anxiety in our relationship."**

---

reflect

In what ways do you manage your freedom to protect your relationship?

....

....

....

....

....

....

COURAGE

You need courage to understand what you are walking into and courage to walk away if it is not what you want.

Someone kept being asked, "Why aren't you married? I can't believe you're not married!" She said, "I'd rather be single than wish I was."

At the completion of this course, typically…

- 4 out of 10 couples decide not to get married
- 2 out of 10 decide to wait
- 4 out of 10 decide to continue and get married

Six out of ten couples change their direction by going through this course!

**The person in front of you
is different from you in so many ways;
You're going to need
COURAGE
to work through those differences.**

---

reflect

Do you have the courage to take an honest look at your relationship throughout this course and walk away if it's not what you want? Explain:

....

....

....

....

....

La La La FACTOR

Love has a lot of emotion and feelings, especially in a new relationship.

The *La La La* factor happens when you are so in love, you aren't thinking clearly. It's like an illusion.

You hear or say things like, "I am in love! I can't stop myself! I just can't live without you! You're everything I ever dreamed of!"

La La La is **not** your friend; You start wanting something so bad that you stop looking at the obvious and run right through all the red flags.

Sheri and I had our first child Brittney a year after we were married. We had a Toyota pickup for our car. Between the seats was the gear shift, the car seat, and a one year old. We thought, "We have to get another car. This is ridiculous!" We decided to go to the car dealership to look around for a nice, four door family car, the kind of cars my grandparents drove. I'm thinking, "This is happening to me. You have got to have four doors so you can get in and out of the car and be able to have access to this child and all of her debris." Suddenly, we go around the corner and see this certain car. The angels sing to me! It was a 1988 Trans Am with 7,000 miles on it! It was only a year old!

I felt Jesus say, "Take it for a test drive Danny." And I say, "Yes Lord. I am but Your servant!" We start it up and took it for a test drive... vroom! The Spirit leapt within me with great joy! We bought it, took it home, had it for seven months until it needed new tires, which were $250 a tire and a new set of brakes for $1,000. My first needed repair on this car and it caused me to trade it in. I was $3,000 upside down. That is La La La right there! My brain stopped working and I fell in love with a hole in the ground.

reflect

Is the *La La La* factor operating in your relationship? If so, what can you do to manage your emotions and take an honest look at your relationship?

....

....

....

....

t ....

CONNECTION

Connection is the goal of relationship.

Anxiety has a great affect on that connection.

You can decrease the anxiety and increase the love.

Love and fear are enemies. They cannot occupy the same space.

Love casts out or chases away fear,

and fear chases away love

As soon as you aren't protecting a fragile relationship, it is going to manifest itself in anxiety and you will disconnect.

When you are in *La La La*, you'll do whatever you have to do to keep hold of your relationship. If you continue doing what ever it takes, you will end up not getting any of your needs meet.

It is important that you learn how to identify your own needs, communicate them, and see the person's response to that on this side of marriage.

If a rope is used as an analogy for connection, anxiety is like dripping acid on the rope. If you don't know what to do about the anxiety created by any situation (whether it is money, children, family members, or is job related, or health related), then you are just dripping acid on the rope. It is fraying, and eventually you are living disconnected and you are only connected by an "I do" that you can't even remember. When you are disconnected in love, your life becomes filled with anxiety. You can decrease the anxiety and increase the love by staying connected.

reflect

Identify and list some of your needs that should be communicated:

....

....

....

....

....

....

....

....

....

....

....

....

SERIES OUTLINE

SESSION ONE | Series Introduction

- An introduction to the Defining the Relationship Series

SESSION TWO | Powerful People, Powerful Decisions

- Learn the difference between powerful and powerless people

- Understand that it takes powerful people to make powerful decisions

- Consider questions that are helpful on this side of "I do"

- Discover what it means to manage yourself and your freedoms to protect your love

SESSION THREE | Living On Purpose

- Discover and define your life's purpose

- Identify what makes you come alive

- Write a mission statement

- Learn what it means to make a commitment and live in commitment

SESSION FOUR | 7 Pillars of a Healthy Relationship

- Learn the structures to build a solid foundation for relationship

- Identify how to protect the peace, joy, and hope in your relationship

- Find out how to increase the love while dealing with fear

This series helped us to solidify that we were making a good choice in each other!

Skyler & Kim

SESSION FIVE | Love Languages

- Discover your love language

- Understand how each other's love language is critical to success in connecting and communicating

- Identify how your love language affects motive, practice, skills, and perception of one another

SESSION SIX | Your "Normal"

- Discuss how you were raised and what has been your "normal"

- Learn what to do when two "normals" come together and create anxiety

- Consider how your "normal" will affect the long-term experience of raising children and creating a new normal

SESSION SEVEN | Communication Dance

- Learn the different styles and levels of communication

- Discover the real meaning of intimacy

- Identify how to communicate effectively what's going on inside of you

SESSION EIGHT | Conflict Management

- Learn a powerful way to resolve conflict

- Work on strengthening and managing yourself on the inside no matter what happens on the outside

- Change the quality of your relationship and the quality of your life

SESSION NINE | 90/10 Factor

- Discuss differences between men and women and what motivates them in relationship

- Learn the cycle of trust that strengthens and brings out the best in both of you

---

**Marriage is like hockey, and this series and
its administrators are the goalie.
Our job is to keep bouncing the puck back to you and
you'll need to decide if the relationship can pass the test.**

---

class exercise

Write down the top three qualities of the person you are with or would like to be with.

....

....

....

Why are these important to you?

....

....

....

What are the top three feelings you enjoy when you are with this person?

....

....

....

Discuss these questions together as a class or in small groups.

1. What do you hope to gain from this class?

2. What topics stand out to you as significant to your relationship?

3. What did you hear in the session that you can apply to your relationship already?

Take some time to communicate as a couple, either after class or during the week.

1. Where are you at now in your relationship?

2. What issues do you want addressed throughout the course?

3. As a couple, in what areas of your relationship do you want to grow the most?

homework

1. **On your own** go back through the session notes and write out your answers to the *Reflect* questions.

2. **Together** discuss the *Communicate* questions and talk through any issues or topics that were brought up during the session.

3. **Journal** your thoughts and dreams as you walk through the journey of this course.

journal

Powerful People
Powerful Decisions

2

Powerful People Powerful Decisions

2

session two

THE POWER TO MAKE A DECISION

MATCHING THE POWERFUL AND POWERLESS

"THERE IS NO *TRY*"

POWERLESS PEOPLE

POWERFUL PEOPLE

WHAT ARE YOU BUILDING?

THE POWER TO MAKE A DECISION

The very essence of love is this, "I choose you!"

Jesus said,
"You did not choose me but I chose you."

John 15:16 (NASB)

- A natural response to a human being who likes you is that you like them back, but that's not a good reason to get married!

 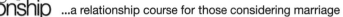

- It's a very powerful act to love someone out of choice. Love must be rooted in this.

- I chose you out of a decision to love you.

reflect

Do you feel that you've been a powerful decision maker in your relationship? If so, how?

....

....

....

....

....

....

MATCHING THE POWERFUL AND POWERLESS

3 Types of Relating

Powerless + Powerless = Controlling
Powerful + Powerless = Dependent
Powerful + Powerful = Free

Powerless & Powerless

- When you match two people together who can't manage themselves, you end up with two people who are very scared and very controlling.

- If I am powerless, I live in a perpetual state of anxiety and fear because I feel out of control of my own life.

- Instead of me managing me, we are trying to manage each other.

Powerful & Powerless

- In this co-dependent relationship, the powerful person is in constant rescue mode for the powerless person.

- The powerless person's success becomes dependent on the powerful person's intervention.

Powerful & Powerful

- Both people are managing themselves.

- I can be me around you. You can be you around me.

- I don't need control of you. You don't need control of me.

- What keeps us tied together is the strength of love we have built.

- Lots of people can create dependency, but only free people can create love.

reflect

Are you taking responsibility for somebody else's life or letting them take responsibility for yours?

....

....

....

What kind of match are you in? Is there anything you would like to change? If so, what?

....

....

....

....

....

We want to become the best versions of ourselves.

Skyler & Kim

19

"THERE IS NO *TRY*"

Voice of Choice

Irresponsible Voice = "I'll try"
Powerless Voice = "I have to" or "I can't"
Powerful Voice = "I will"

Powerless people believe the lie that they cannot manage their own lives.

- Powerless people require others to "make" them happy and carry no personal responsibility toward meeting their own needs for contentment, hope, and love.

- Do you manage your "happy," or do you need a "happy" manager?

- "I'll try" is a poor effort to convince somebody that you're going to do something; it's rooted in powerlessness.

Powerful people are willing to take responsibility for their decisions.

- A powerful person says, "I will," "I do," and "I am."

- Being powerful requires truth, integrity, and responsibility.

- Listen to your language. If you don't know if you are powerful or not, listen to your response to requirements, demands, and challenges.

reflect

Do you use phrases like, *"I'll try"* or *"I can't"* very often? How is that affecting your choice-making skills?

....

....

....

POWERLESS PEOPLE

Powerless People

Are famous for blaming others
Are scared of many things and want control
Require other people to 'make' them happy

Powerless people give other people the credit for being powerful rather than themselves.

- They create environments that have a lot of anxiety.

- They blame others for the life they have.

- They have a victim mentality.

- Victims are caught in the same problems over and over, because they do not take responsibility for their own life.

- Everywhere you go, there you are again.

reflect

Is what you had hoped to avoid being recreated around you? Have you been living with a *"victim"* **mentality? If so, how?**

....

....

....

....

....

....

POWERFUL PEOPLE

Powerful People

Create respectful and responsible relationships; Happen to live rather than to react to it
Set limits with abuse or disrespectful people; Direct the choices and decision in their life
Manage themselves regardless of what others do.

Powerful people will not only take responsibility for today, but also for tomorrow. They know the decisions they make today will create the tomorrow they're going to live in.

- They don't just attract who they want, but who they are.

- Their relationships happen from the inside out.

- Their environment does not affect them; they affect their environment.

- They know how to set limits with people who have no value for what they're doing.

- They are a volunteer, not a victim!
  II Timothy 1:7 *"For God has not given us a spirit of fear, but of power and of love and of a sound mind."* (NKJV)

- They can direct their own life and vision, because they have a mind that gives them the ability to manage themselves.

- Their love is not dependent on being loved back.

reflect

Are you affecting your environment more than your environment is affecting you? Explain.

....

....

....

WHAT ARE YOU BUILDING?

When you consider marrying someone, they must know how to build a life where the people around them are powerful, loving, honoring, and respectful people.

What the other person is building is what you are going to come into, so pay attention!

**The goal of a healthy relationship
is two fully alive people joining together
to make a life neither one could have by them self.**

Imagine you have a business that's making lots of money, and another business owner comes up to you and says, "Hey, we should put our businesses together!" You ask, "Really? Well, is your business thriving?" "Oh yeah," the other says, "I just painted my new truck! All new paint!" "Great! What's in the truck?" you ask. "Oh you know, just some stuff - stuff I sell." "How much stuff do you have?" "Oh, just one. Actually I'm kind of broke, and I was really hoping to hook onto your life and pour some of your resources into my business, because I'm terrible at it." Are you going to say, "Yeah, I'd love to do that!" No way! A good business owner isn't going to join with that guy in a million years! Are you a good owner of your life and relationships?

reflect

Consider the person you are attracted to: Are they capable of building their own life? Can you see yourself being a part of what they're building? Are YOU capable of building your own life? Explain.

....

....

....

Discuss these questions together as a class or in small groups.

1. Who would you say was more powerful in your parent's marriage and what did that look like?

2. Can you think of a married couple you really look up to where both people in the relationship are powerful? Give examples of what it looks like.

3. Do you think a powerless person can realistically become powerful and if so, what things could they do to become powerful?

4. What role does knowing your identity play in being powerful in your relationships?

5. Has the word *"powerful"* had a bad connotation for you in the past? How?

Take some time to communicate as a couple, either after class or during the week.

1. What do you value about the other person in your relationship? Do you have a strong connection? Are you simply strung together by the *"La La La" factor*?

2. What did you learn as a child about decision making? Was somebody else responsible for your decisions? Do you feel like a *powerful* or *powerless* person in your relationship? What do you need to grow in that area?

3. How can you help each other to both be powerful in this relationship?

1. **On your own** go back through the session notes and write out your answers to the *Reflect* questions.

2. **Together** discuss the *Communicate* questions and talk through any issues or topics that were brought up during the session.

3. **Journal** your thoughts and dreams as you walk through the journey of this course.

journal

Living
On Purpose

3

Living On Purpose

3

session three

DESTINATION
ACTIVITY: WRITING A MISSION STATEMENT
COMPASS: POINTING TRUE NORTH
TAKING A LOOK AT YOUR MISSION

DESTINATION

Destination starts with you as the individual moving toward a vision.

> **A man without a vision
> is a man without a future,
> and a man without a future
> will always return to his past**

Many people get caught up in what HAS happened because their life isn't pointed at what they're building.

You as a couple, as a married couple, need to be searching or working toward a clear destination.

Think about when you are 85 years old sitting on the front porch of your house with your spouse in your rocking chair, or on the tennis court, or doing whatever you're doing at 85. Have this conversation, "What did we accomplish with our life together?" Answer it there and then back up to today and build toward that.

It's like the headlights on your car. Your mission for life is as far as your headlights go. As your car moves, you see new things. The faster you're moving, the faster new things are coming into your vision. Get bright lights, see as far as you possibly can, and stay active in what it is that you're building and you're pointing your life at.

Then the LORD answered me and said,
"Record the vision And inscribe it on tablets,
That the one who reads it may run.
For the vision is yet for the appointed time;
It hastens toward the goal and it will not fail.
Though it tarries, wait for it;
For it will certainly come, it will not delay."

Habakuk 2:2-3 NASB

There is a destination that has been planted in you by the very purposes of God.

- Your destination is looking for you. Stay true to it. Stay true to your passion.

- It is important that you get together with another powerful person who is pointing himself or herself at a destination.

- When you have two powerful people whose visions don't line up, one of you will have to shut off your vision to protect the relationship.

reflect

Where are you going? What is your destination?

....

....

....

....

....

....

Has your destination changed?

....

....

....

....

....

What do you want to accomplish in your lifetime?

....

....

....

....

....

 Writing a Mission Statement
adapted from Laurie Beth Jones' book, *The Path*

1. Choose ten words, from the **VERBS** below, that best describe the movement and effect of your life. Choose words you gravitate toward the most. Write them down.

....

....

VERBS

advance	dance	free	move	remind	succeed
advise	dare	gaze	offer	remove	sway
allow	decide	give	open	render	talk
arrange	deliver	have	order	require	taste
ask	direct	heal	pay	restore	teach
beg	discover	hear	permit	reveal	tell
believe	draw	help	persuade	revive	think
breathe	dream	hire	plan	run	translate
bring	empower	hope	play	say	travel
build	encourage	instruct	point	search	try
buy	examine	invite	pray	see	understand
carry	exist	kneel	preach	send	urge
challenge	expect	lead	prepare	serve	use
change	explain	lean	promise	shake	wait
choose	express	learn	quake	shoot	want
clean	facilitate	leave	read	smile	warn
command	feel	let	rebuild	spend	wish
complete	find	like	receive	stand	work
confound	finish	listen	reconcile	start	write
confront	fix	live	recover	stay	
connect	fly	love	redeem	stimulate	
console	follow	make	refuse	stop	
create	forbid	meet	release	strive	
cut	force	motivate	remember	study	

2. From the list of ten, narrow it down to three words. These are the ones that **MOST** describe the activity of your life.

....

....

3. Choose five words, from the **SERVICES** below, that best describe your talents and desire to serve others. If the service word that best describes you is not on the list, write it in.

- What is the service of your life? What strengths do you have?
- What is the manifestation of your gifts, your talent, your calling, and your anointing?
- How will your life serve and benefit the people around you?

....

....

....

SERVICES

Administering	Exhortation	Prayer
Aiding	Feeding	Prophecy
Art	Giving	Reading
Building	Harvest	Revival
Business	Healing	Running
Cleaning	Health	Salvation
Comforting	Hospitality	Serving
Cooking	Intercession	Sewing
Counsel	Leading	Singing
Dancing	Love	Supporter
Deliverance	Massage	Teaching
Dental	Medicine	Transportation
Economics	Mercy	Working
Education	Music	Worship
Entertain	Organizing	Writing
Evangelism	Planning	
Excellence	Politics	

4. From the list of five, narrow it down to no more than two services to others.

....

....

....

5. Choose up to three words, from the **TARGETS** below, that best describe your life's work and attention. If you don't find your target on the list, write it in.

- Who are you aiming your life at? Who will benefit most from the service of your life?

- Think about where you are most drawn. Are you drawn to: the political system, a specific people group, or a certain system like social welfare or economics? Are you drawn to a region or profession? Who is the target of your life?

....

....

TARGET GROUPS OR AREAS

Abused	Eternity	Political System
Africa	Europe	Poor
All peoples	Family Systems	Possessed
America	First Nations	Pre-believers
Artists	People	Relationships
Asia	Heaven	Religious System
Asians	Hispanics	Saved
Athletes	Hungry	Searching
Sick	Hurting	Single
Blacks	Illiterate	Social Services
Broken	Legal System	Systems
Business World	Lonely	South America
Children	Lost	Systems
Church	Married	Terminally ill
Cities	Medical/Science	Under privileged
Civil Systems	System	Violent offenders
Criminals	Men	Weak
Divorced	Mission Field	Wealthy
Earth	Musicians	Women
Economic System	Needy	Wounded
Education System	Neglected	
Entrepreneurs	Oppressed	

6. From the list of three, narrow it down to one word.

- The clarity of the target helps define the clarity of your life.

....

....

7. Write down your completed list of:

Three Verbs: _____

Two Services: _____

One Target: _____

8. Using your completed list of words, write them into a sentence.

"My mission in life is to..." or *"My purpose in life is to..."*

....

....

Example:

"My mission in life is to free, reconcile, and inspire all peoples of the Earth through prayer and revival."

This activity helps you create a statement of why you get out of bed in the morning.

**Creating a purpose statement or a mission statement
is a way to confront yourself
concerning the direction of your life**

COMPASS: Pointing True North

A mission statement is like building a compass. It has a true north.

- If you don't have a compass, you'll think the direction you're going is your destiny.

- Keep your Mission Statement in front of you and every time you have a decision, check your compass.

- Ask yourself, "Is this decision leading me due north?"

- These things aren't in cement; they can change.

We are building a legacy. We want to leave an imprint of ourselves on this earth.

Skyler & Kim

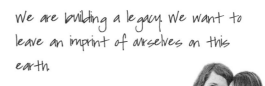

It's important that you know why you're alive.

In the pursuit of where it is that you're going and who it is you're becoming, you meet someone along the way.

Parents often ask, "What are you doing? Where are you going with your life?"

TAKING A LOOK AT YOUR MISSION

The two Mission Statements can be a source of anxiety for some relationships.

- You just identified the tension that these two very different directions are going to create.

- Invite other people into your life whose input you value and have given a place of government in your life.

- Place them there to help you make decisions and trust their input and counsel.

- You are not an island.

- One thing you should be asking yourself when you are making a decision to spend the rest of your lives together is, "How will we negotiate these places of tension beforehand?"

- If you buy a house, you get a full disclosure statement. The person who owns the house has to tell you EVERYTHING that's going on with the house, not just the good stuff.

- You have to be willing to take on the responsibility of the other person, good and bad, and realize there may be a point of anxiety when the point of tension comes up.

Discuss these questions together as a class or in small groups.

1. What is the future you are expecting to step into?

2. Share your mission statement. What came up as you were creating your mission statement? How can it help you?

3. What are you doing with your life that points you in the direction of your destiny?

Take some time to communicate as a couple, either after class or during the week.

1. Look at each other's mission statements. Do they align? Are they similar destinations? In what ways?

2. Create a Mission Statement for you as a couple.

3. What things in your life aren't pointing you to your mission? Are there things that can be cut out?

1. **On your own** go back through the session notes and write out your answers to the *Reflect* questions.

2. **Together** discuss the *Communicate* questions and talk through any issues or topics that were brought up during the session.

3. **Journal** your thoughts and dreams as you walk through the journey of this course.

7 Pillars of
HEALTHY RELATIONSHIPS

4

7 Pillars of HEALTHY RELATIONSHIPS 4

session four

UNCONDITIONAL ACCEPTANCE

THE 7 PILLARS

> **PILLAR ONE** | LOVE
>
> **PILLAR TWO** | HONOR
>
> **PILLAR THREE** | SELF-CONTROL
>
> **PILLAR FOUR** | RESPONSIBILITY
>
> **PILLAR FIVE** | TRUTH
>
> **PILLAR SIX** | FAITH
>
> **PILLAR SEVEN** | VISION

PROTECTING THE VALUE WITHIN

Wisdom has built her house;
She has hewn out her seven pillars.

Proverbs 9:1

UNCONDITIONAL ACCEPTANCE

A marriage is held together by the strength of its internal structure.

- The ability of any structure to withstand the forces of nature is rooted in the engineering of the infrastructure.

- There aren't many external forces pressuring you to stay married.

- A marriage is held together by what is on the inside.

- If you don't create a plan from the beginning to build something that lasts, then you won't have something that lasts at all.

"I have more hope for people who are going through marriage problems than anybody I know. I've watched the Lord do this from the inside out. Sheri and I getting together was like an earthquake and a tsunami! Between our families, there are fifteen marriages! It happened against all odds, against external forces, against family history, against temperament matches, and anything else you could possibly set out there."

Unconditional acceptance is the foundation of healthy relationships.

- Unconditional acceptance says that though you are very different, I accept who you are.

- "You get to be you and I get to be me."

- I accept the fact that I can't control you and you can't control me.

The goal is not to make you into me or to gain control over you, but to build a relationship that is strong enough that we manage ourselves to protect our connection.

Out of all the freedoms I have, I make different choices because I know that some of them affect you.

- The Lord is not looking to control us, either. It's not His job to manage your relationship with Him.

- He is looking at how you value His needs.

- It's not my job to manage your love towards me. It's my job to manage my love towards you.

reflect

Where have you felt free to be who you are? At home? At school? At work? What made it feel that way?

....

....

....

....

....

The biggest pillar for us is truth.

Skyler & Kim

THE SEVEN PILLARS

PILLAR ONE | Love

Love means this: "I feel connected. I feel safe. I feel nourished."

- If there's not an intimate connection, it isn't love.

- The pillar of love is rooted in fearlessness.

- Love is not about dependency.

- Love chases away the fear and the anxiety.

PILLAR TWO | Honor

Honor is about two powerful people in a relationship working together to meet the needs of one another. When your definition of honor is, "I have all the power and you have no power," you have created fear for the relationship.

- The result of being overpowered is anxiety and fear.

- God has honored us and changed us from servant to friend. What kind of power do you have over your friends? You don't. Friendships are held together by love and by the way we treat each other, not by controlling one another.

- **John 15:15** *"I no longer call you servants, because a servant does not know his master's business. Instead, I have called you friends..."* (NIV)

- Honor is not about surrendering all your power. Honor is about being powerful.

We are co-laborers with God, not sub-contractors. We are co-heirs with Christ:

- Everything that Jesus inherited from the Father, we inherit too!

- We now have two powerful people co-laboring. We have to act with less fear and more respect, more love.

reflect

What does love look like to you? Does it appear fragile, weak, or simply a way to put up with each other? Or does it look like an intimate, nourishing connection? Explain.

Do you see yourself as God's servant or as His friend? Why?

PILLAR THREE | Self Control

II Timothy 1:7 *"For God gave us a spirit not of fear but of power and love and self-control."* (ESV)

- I can tell myself what to do, and I'm responsible to do that very thing.

- It's my job to manage me, no matter what you do.

- I have the ability to choose a goal of a loving, intimate connection with my spouse.

- I cannot blame you for how I am behaving towards you. You are never in charge of how I treat you; I am.

PILLAR FOUR | Responsibility

Responsibility is my ability to respond to life.

- Am I prepared to deal with my life and my decisions?

- My goal is my responsibility. Your goal is your responsibility. I don't control your efforts on your goal. You don't control my efforts on my goal.

- In relationships, you must have a plan for how you are going to respond, no matter what anybody else does and no matter what happens.

- Responsibility says, "I have a plan."

reflect

How has self-control been evident in your life?

Does what people do dictate how you respond? Why?

....

....

....

....

....

PILLAR FIVE | Truth

Truth is a form of trust, and trust is the exchange of truth.

- Trust cannot be rooted in my desire for you to be as much like me as possible.

- I tell you the truth by telling you what's going on inside of me.

- When you have really good information about me, you are able to make much better decisions.

- You don't handle or control my trust. I do. I trust whoever I want to, and I don't trust whoever I want to.

- When God doesn't do what people think He should have done, they don't trust Him. Does that mean God's not trustworthy?

- If we cannot trust the Perfect One, how easy is it to not trust people? Jesus deepened His covenant with the disciples on the night He knew they were going to betray Him. He didn't stop being Himself simply because of their behavior or character.

- Classically, we don't tell each other the truth and are guarded, protecting ourselves, but trust is constructed in the exchange of truth.

PILLAR SIX | Faith

Faith says that you have a supernatural resource for your relationship.

- If your relationship doesn't have somebody to answer to, then the strong man will win.

- If we have faith and somebody to answer to, then we are governed in this relationship. It's not all up to us.

- When I'm answering to God and He is the master of our marriage, it changes the way we make decisions.

- *Instruction* means, "I can have structure built into me. People on the outside can instruct me, and I will respond and function according to the structure that's inside of me."

Are you able to receive instruction through your faith? In what ways?

What is the necessary prerequisite before you allow yourself to trust someone? Why is that your standard and where did it come from?

....

....

....

PILLAR SEVEN | Vision

Having vision for your life will help determine whether you have a destiny together.

- In your relationship, you must know what it is that you are constructing.

- Do you have a destiny and a destination together, or are you just working together side by side until you drift apart?

- People drift apart when they plan different destinies or fail to plan a common destination.

- Vision will allow you to create and construct an environment together.

reflect

What is it that your relationship is constructing? Do you have a destiny and a destination together?

....

....

....

PROTECTING THE VALUE WITHIN

Whoever has no rule over his own spirit is like
a city broken down, without walls.

Proverbs 25:28

- In Bible days, a city was protected from looters, marauders, and armies by its walls. It was the only thing protecting the city's health, value, and well-being. Only people who respect what's in there can enter.

- You can build all these pillars, but if you don't understand what it takes to live a life of protecting them, then you'll give them away.

- The core of your life is about being free, and Jesus thought it was worth dying for!

- The only way I'm going to be able to live a life of integrity and protect the value inside of me is if I learn how to set limits to outside forces.

- External forces can come against me day or night, but they will stay on the outside, while I stay free on the inside.

- Your rule over your own spirit is imperative for having healthy relationships.

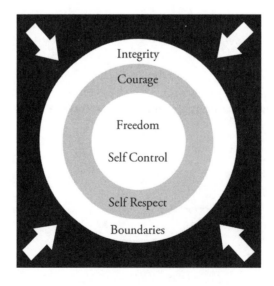

reflect

How have you protected the value inside of you? How have boundaries and healthy limits been a part of your life?

....

....

....

....

They suddenly recognize that God is a living, personal presence,
not a piece of chiseled stone.

And when God is personally present, a living Spirit, that old,
constricting legislation is recognized as obsolete. We're free of it!

II Corinthians 3:17 (The Message Bible)

  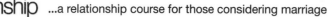

Discuss these questions together as a class or in small groups.

1. What are two things that stood out to you from today's teaching?

2. Which of the seven pillars do you think is your strongest? Why?

3. Which of the seven pillars needs to be strengthened? Why? Write them down.

Take some time to communicate as a couple, either after class or during the week.

1. What are the main pillars that are particularly important in your life and relationship?

2. What pillars in your lives and your relationships need strengthening? What practical actions can you take to see that happen?

3. How is integrity evident in your lives?

4. How have you protected the value of what's on the inside of you? How have you protected the value of the other person in the relationship?

5. What healthy boundaries have been set in your relationship? Do you need to add any more?

6. Discuss how your relationship is held together. Are there any external pressures coming against you or are you building together from the inside out?

homework

1. **On your own** go back through the session notes and write out your answers to the *Reflect* questions.

2. **Together** discuss the *Communicate* questions and talk through any issues or topics that were brought up during the session.

3. **Journal** your thoughts and dreams as you walk through the journey of this course.

journal

Love
LANGUAGES

5

Love LANGUAGES 5

session five

THE GOAL OF YOUR RELATIONSHIP

THE BEST-KEPT SECRET

LANGUAGES OF LOVE

    ONE | GIFTS

    TWO | TOUCH

    THREE | ACTS OF SERVICE

    FOUR | WORDS OF AFFIRMATION

    FIVE | QUALITY TIME

"I LOVE YOU VERY MUCH"

THE GOAL OF YOUR RELATIONSHIP

As you learn to send the message "I love you very much," the strength of the bond you have will increase every day.

- When something unexpected comes up and tests our connection, the belief that you love me very much is already resident in me.

What is the goal of your relationship?
A safe distance or an intimate, loving connection?

- When you change your goal from connection to distance, it leads only to destruction.

- Nobody can change your goal but you.

- The goal must be love, especially when you are disconnected.

Teacher, which is the greatest commandment
in the Law? Jesus replied,
"Love the Lord your God with all your heart
and with all your soul and with all your mind."
This is the first and greatest commandment.
And the second is like it:
Love your neighbor as yourself.

Matthew 22:36-39 (NIV)

The greatest thing you can do as a believer is to LOVE.

- Do you know what it takes to love and to lay down your life?

- Loving well is an inside job. Nothing on the outside is going to make you love well.

- Loving well takes determination, intention, and practice.

- It's easy to love people who love you back, but it's a real challenge to love someone who doesn't love you back.

reflect

Can you think of a time when you changed your goal in a relationship from connection to distance? What happened? How can you maintain your goal regardless of relational circumstances?

....

....

....

THE BEST-KEPT SECRET

Unfortunately, one of the best-kept secrets in families today is, "I love you" and, "I value our relationship."

Greater love has no one than this,
than to lay down one's life for his friends.

John 15:13 (NKJV)

- I change my goal from connection to distance when I withhold, "I love you very much."

- People will hear "I love you" in very different ways, and you need to know what love language they speak so there won't be a language barrier.

"Men and women are very different when it comes to expressing love. Imagine a Russian man marrying a Japanese woman. On the night of their honeymoon, the Russian man decides he is going to woo his wife with beautiful Russian poetry. So he jumps out of the bathroom and blurts out Russian poetry! She's thinking, 'What is he mad about?' She's not quite getting the message he's sending, because he's speaking a different language. It doesn't matter how intentional he is about it or how true it is, she doesn't understand him. Later on, she comes out in her kimono with her little tray and incense. And he's going, 'Are we going to eat that or are you going to play with that?' He doesn't have a grid for it! It doesn't mean anything to him. Even though they're both trying so hard, they're both going to break down in frustration because they don't know how each other receives love."

We tend to speak our native language. It is easy to send the message "I love you" by the way we best receive it.

**Laying down your life so that somebody feels
and experiences love is like learning a new language.**

---

reflect

Was "I love you" a secret in your family growing up? How about now? What steps can you take
to ensure that love and value are not secrets in the family that you create?

....

....

....

....

....

....

....

....

....

LANGUAGES OF LOVE

Adapted from Gary Chapman's book, *The Five Love Languages: How To Express Heartfelt Commitment To Your Mate*

ONE | Gifts

Connection: "You know me and were thinking about me when I wasn't even around!"

- Gift shows that you were thinking about this person while you were away from each other

- Gift shows that you know them and know how to affirm that about them

- Gift shows that you remembered a special occasion, which could be any occasion, to express your love

Disconnection: "You don't care because you don't even know me or give me a passing thought."

- Forget the gift

- Poor gift selection

- Miss a special occasion

A person with the ***gift*** love language, feels connected through the expression of a gift that represents that you know them and understand them.

- It's not about money or diamonds or gold, but about knowing and thinking about them.

- Life and death is in the power of the gift.

reflect

Do you experience love and connection through gifts? Where have you noticed or experienced this love language before and what happened? Who do you know with this love language?

....

....

....

TWO | Touch

Connection: "I feel connected when we are touching."

- Physical contact

- Physical proximity

- Contact frequency

Disconnection: "I feel rejected and neglected when you don't touch me."

- Missed opportunities for touching

- Neglecting public displays of affection (PDA's)

- Extended periods of time between touches

A person with **touch** love language, feels connected when touching or being touched by others.

- Touch love language people are designed with a meter in their chest that is counting the seconds since they were last touched.

- Anxiety increases if they go for long periods of time without some sort of affection or physical touch.

- Touch love language people are looking for opportunities to touch. If you don't take the opportunity, that hurts!

reflect

Do you experience love and connection through touch? Where have you noticed or experienced this love language before and what happened? Who do you know with this love language?

....

....

....

....

....

THREE | Acts of Service

Connection: "I feel loved when you take care of things that are important to me."

- Doing things for them

- Anticipating needs and meeting them

- Accomplishing specific tasks

Disconnection: "You don't care about me, because you don't care about things that are important to me."

- Neglect "help me" messages

- Angry responses to doing tasks

- Do tasks unrelated to request or need

People with *acts of service* love language, feel loved when you help by doing something that is important to them.

- When you do something for them that is important to them, it communicates the message that you value them and what's important to them.

- Uncompleted tasks create anxiety for them. When they look around a messy room, their anxiety is building because they feel that nobody is going to do anything about it but them.

- You lower their anxiety by helping them.

- The kiss of death for this love language is "Don't tell me what to do! I'm not your slave!"

- When you don't take care of things that are important to them, you send the message that they are not important to you.

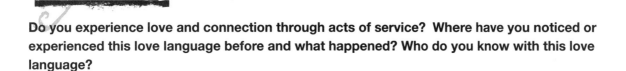

Do you experience love and connection through acts of service? Where have you noticed or experienced this love language before and what happened? Who do you know with this love language?

....

....

FOUR | Words of Affirmation

Connection: "I feel loved when I believe that you like me."

- Words are life!

- Words contain value for who I am

- Words say – "I believe in you!"

Disconnection: "I feel rejected when your words are harsh."

- Criticism slays them

- Super-sensitive to disapproval and/or correction

- Extended spans of time without value messages

People with *words of affirmation* love language, feel loved when you express it to them in words.

- "Life and death is in the power of the tongue!"

- These people need to feel enjoyed and liked.

- They will have a very hard time with anger, criticism, and negativity.

- When confronting people with a words of affirmation love language, use a "Hero Sandwich." *For example:* "I love you very much; this thing you're doing is not working at all; I love you very much."

- Saying "I love you" is very important to them.

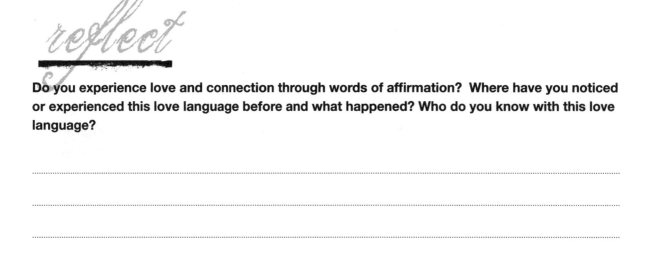

Do you experience love and connection through words of affirmation? Where have you noticed or experienced this love language before and what happened? Who do you know with this love language?

....

....

....

FIVE | Quality Time

Connection: "I feel loved when you show interest in me."

- Sharing in an activity or conversation that is important to them

- Listening with symptoms of being engaged in the conversation

- Willing participation in their interests or hobbies

Disconnection: "I feel rejected when you don't value my interests."

- Be distracted or uninterested

- Fail to listen well

- Fail to make time for connecting with them

The person with *quality time* love language, feels loved when you invest your time and interest into them.

- Quality time love language people need to feel interesting to you no matter what they are talking about or what they are doing.

- They feel valued and loved when you show interest.

- Spending time together is about love, not the activity itself.

- The kiss of death is this: "I don't have time; I'm busy; I don't care; I don't listen well; I disengage."

- When you send the message to them that you are not interested in what they are talking about, they experience that as you not being interested in them.

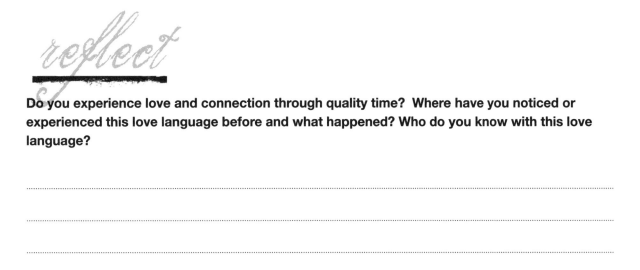

Do you experience love and connection through quality time? Where have you noticed or experienced this love language before and what happened? Who do you know with this love language?

....

....

....

"I LOVE YOU VERY MUCH"

You may have to learn new languages for saying "I love you very much" according to how your spouse receives it best.

- Be careful when you and your significant other have the same love language; be sure that you're not just "petting" yourself.

- There isn't a better feeling than effectively communicating the message "I love you very much" to the person you love so much.

- Simply learning what love feels like to your spouse and your family and doing it will chase away fear.

- You are my target; God is my source.

reflect

How do you feel when a person effectively communicates to you that they love you? What does that look like?

....

....

....

....

....

....

We choose to make the time to learn each other's love language.

Skyler & Kim

Discuss these questions together as a class or in small groups.

1. What points in this lesson stood out to you and why?

2. How does having a goal of connection in mind help your relationship?

3. Share your different love languages. Discuss what it looks like for you to successfully receive the "I love you" message.

4. Can you think of any other love languages that you have experienced?

Take some time to communicate as a couple, either after class or during the week.

1. Discuss your family life growing up. How often was the message, "I love you," communicated? How did that affect you?

2. What love languages are most applicable to each of you individually? Give examples of ways you've felt loved through this language before.

1. **On your own** go back through the session notes and write out your answers to the *Reflect* questions.

2. **Together** discuss the *Communicate* questions and talk through any issues or topics that were brought up during the session.

3. **Journal** your thoughts and dreams as you walk through the journey of this course.

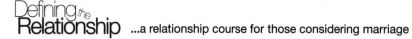

journal

Your
"NORMAL"

6

Your "NORMAL"

6

session six

FAMILY TEMPLATES
OLD vs NEW
LADIES & GENTLEMEN

FAMILY TEMPLATES

It's a challenge to create something from what you've never seen before.

- Your DNA and the environment you grew up in are powerful in how you live today.

- They are not determiners; they are influencers. They create unique challenges for you.

- If you don't shift your family template, the family dynamics that you experienced will be repeated throughout the course of your life.

- The skills and behavior patterns that are handed to you from your family will affect the way you think, the way you decide, and the way you react.

"I didn't even know a Christian until I was 17 years old. I didn't get saved until I was 21, and Sheri didn't get saved until she was 21. In our two family trees we have multiple divorces, addiction, alcoholism, imprisonment, domestic violence, and all kinds of stuff going on. This was our normal. Now we take all this momentum and we create our own family. There were a number of places where this could have all come apart and ended. It took 13 and a half years before our marriage turned around, and now we have a completely different second half of our lives together, because we learned to live differently than what we were handed."

Quick Inventory

- How did you relate to your other gender parent as a teenager?

- Trust?

- Honor?

- Self-control?

- Connection or distance?

- How would you rate your relationship now?

reflect

What does your family template look like? How did you experience trust? Could you tell the truth? Could you be yourself? Was there an expression of honor? Were you powerful or powerless? Was it your responsibility to make your mom or dad happy? Was the family goal distance or connection? Did you learn how to practice intimacy?

....

....

....

....

OLD vs NEW

The Old Testament dynamic allows the Destroyer to continue bringing the same ruin to each succeeding generation of a family line.

- The sins of the father will visit the children's children's children.

- The destroyer tries to make past avenues of sin a family normal for you.

- We use the tools that we are given and then train our children the same way.

- Usually it takes somebody outside of your family tree to point out an influence that you picked up and made part of your "normal" without even knowing it.

The New Testament promises that you can be transformed by the renewing of your mind.

- Romans 12:2 (NASB) *"And do not be conformed to this world, but be transformed by the renewing of your mind, so that you may prove what the will of God is, that which is good and acceptable and perfect."*

- You no longer have to conform to the patterns of this world; you are introduced to a new world by having access to heaven!

And even now the ax is laid to the root of the trees.
Therefore every tree which does not bear good fruit
is cut down and thrown into the fire.
Luke 3:9 (NKJV)

You no longer have to be stuck in the template you were handed.

- Make it a priority to invite input into your life.

- Your family can be completely different than the family you were raised in.

- You have an opportunity to change the template.

reflect

What destructive "normals" have been wreaking havoc on successive generations of your family? How can you break them and establish a new family template?

....

....

....

....

....

LADIES & GENTLEMEN

Teachability in a man and vulnerability in a woman are vital when looking for a spouse.

- Ladies, make sure your man has someone that can speak into his life.

- Men, a woman's willingness to trust you, believe in you, follow you, and be vulnerable with you is what makes you feel like a man. Make sure she practices intimacy, not distance.

The ability to form a non-sexual soul tie is something you want to look for in your potential husband or wife.

- Look at the relationships going on in your potential spouse's life. Does he/she have evidence of other covenant relationships going on?

- Ladies, if the only way your guy knows how to experience intimacy is through sex, you will find yourself being pressured for it.

- A non-sexual engagement creates a template for serving one another without selfish motivation or manipulation.

- God is all about setting you up for an abundant life with a fresh new template. Don't wait to start renewing that template!

We had two very different normals — now we're coming together and creating a brand new normal that will be our legacy

Skyler & Kim

reflect

Considering these important qualities Danny has mentioned, does your significant other have them? If not, are they willing to work on them? Explain.

....

....

....

....

....

Discuss these questions together as a class or in small groups.

1. What are some "normals" that you recognize growing up with?

2. What does renewing of the mind look like for you? What part does the Lord play in that process?

3. What are ways you can tell that somebody has covenant relationships in their life?

4. Why is having a non-sexual soul tie before marriage so important?

Take some time to communicate as a couple, either after class or during the week.

1. Discussing and discovering your family "normals" will save you both a lot of potential confusion and distress. What was life like at home? Who was in charge, if anybody? What were your traditions, activities, and communication styles? Share fun quirks, too!

2. What people have you allowed to speak into your lives, both individually and as a couple? How strong is their influence?

3. What do you want your family template and "normals" to look like?

1. **On your own** go back through the session notes and write out your answers to the *Reflect* questions.

2. **Together** discuss the *Communicate* questions and talk through any issues or topics that were brought up during the session.

3. **Journal** your thoughts and dreams as you walk through the journey of this course.

journal

Communication
DANCE

7

Communication DANCE

7

session seven

CHANGING OUR GOAL
THE IMPORTANCE OF INTIMACY
COMMUNICATION STYLES
LEVELS OF COMMUNICATION
THE "I" MESSAGES

CHANGING OUR GOAL

Communication can either build or destroy a relationship.

- Often we misperceive what we are familiar with, because we judge it too quickly.

- Assuming you know something is one of the biggest obstacles to healthy communication.

Classically, communication is about convincing you to agree with me, but this requires one person to disappear when we disagree.

- When agreement is the goal, we are only allowing one person into the conversation, because only one of us can be right, and we fight over which one that is.

The Goal of Communication is...

- To Convince?

- To Agree?

- To Understand!

The goal of communication is to UNDERSTAND.

- There is more than one way to see everything.

- When I listen and try to understand you, I am sending you the message that you are valuable and have influence in our relationship.

reflect

Looking back on your life, what goal has most often driven the communication in your relationships?

....

....

....

....

....

THE IMPORTANCE OF INTIMACY

And they were both naked, the man and his wife,
and were not ashamed.

Genesis 2:25 (NKJV)

What we're trying to build is a loving, intimate connection.

- Communication will either stimulate or annihilate the development of that connection.

- When I am vulnerable, I have the opportunity to feel acceptance.

Defining "intimacy"

In-to-Me-see
Safety
Vulnerability
Acceptance

- Feeling completely known, safe, and accepted in your vulnerability brings euphoria to human beings, because we were designed for intimacy and freedom.

- Fear, distance, and self-preservation create an experience that was never a part of God's heart.

For God has not given us a spirit of fear,
but of power and of love and of a sound mind.

II Timothy 1:7 (NKJV)

Intimacy's Counterfeit: Addiction
"An attempt to create intimacy through a relationship with an object"

- Intimacy is so woven into our beings that Satan uses counterfeits like alcohol, drugs, pornography, food, etc. to give you a relationship with something that you can control.

- Addictions happen when people are in pain and can't find the euphoria of true intimacy. They begin to self-medicate.

- If you don't know how to create and protect intimacy in your relationships, then you will have a growing pain, where you are looking for self-medication.

reflect

Have you ever experienced the euphoria of vulnerable intimacy? What was it like? Have you ever used something other than intimacy in relationship to satiate your needs? What was it like?

....

....

....

....

....

....

COMMUNICATION STYLES

Passive Communication : "You matter. I don't"

- The human being who uses this form of communication seems to have no needs and is the eternal long-sufferer. They hide behind a facade, because they're afraid of what will happen if they tell you the truth.

Aggressive Communication   "I matter. You don't"

- This is the T-Rex form of communication! Like the passive communicator, they are also motivated by fear.

Passive Aggressive Communication   "You matter - NOT!"

- This is the worst of both worlds. Sarcastic innuendos, veiled threats, manipulative use of Scripture, and judgements that come in the form of counsel are some signs of   passive aggressive communication.

Assertive Communication   "You matter, and so do I."

- We protect the value of both parties in this style of communication. There are two powerful people involved. Assertive communication increases the love, and is the foundation for mutual respect in a relationship.

Fear & Love Are Mortal Enemies!

There is no fear in love.
But perfect love drives out fear,
because fear has to do with punishment.

I John 4:18 (NIV)

The first three communication styles increase fear in a relationship.

I manage how I relate to everyone that I communicate with.

If people use fearful communication styles against me, they will run into a boundary until they are ready for respectful communication.

reflect

What communication style is most prevalent in your life? How has this affected the well-being of your relationships?

....

....

....

....

LEVELS OF COMMUNICATION

Cliche'
Facts
Opinions/Ideas/Perspective
Feelings
Needs

- Cliches are the beginning level of communication. "How are you?" "Fine, how are you?" "Fine." This requires no communication skills or relationship.

- Facts are used when there is no conflict involved, because differences of opinion aren't involved. "Good morning." "Good morning." "Coffee?" "Please." "Sugar?" "Yes."

- The test of your communication skills is when you have two people show up in the conversation and where the conflict begins.

- Making *understanding* the goal of communication acknowledges the fact that there are two people involved who are experiencing the same situation differently.

"Sheri does not enjoy the ride up Buckhorn Mountain on the way to Weaverville, California like I do. When I'm driving, I am in that car just flying through those corners, loving every second of it, passing every car I can catch up to - it is marvelous! Sheri, on the other hand, is having a completely different experience of this whole thing. I don't understand. I'm a good driver. I should've been a Nascar driver! I've never been in an accident. Why are you scared? You have absolutely no evidence of me being a bad driver. You should just calm down and be like me. How'd that work out for me? Not very well, because she's not going to agree with me. She's not me. She's her. And trying to convince somebody that their feelings aren't valid is like saying, 'You can't be hungry, because I'm not hungry!' How silly is that?"

- When we respond to somebody's heart with our head, we hurt them.

- When I learn how to value your experience of this moment, I'm teaching you that it is safe to show me your heart.

- The holy grail of communication is finding out what it is that you need, and meeting that need.

- Intimacy feels like you are loved and cared about.

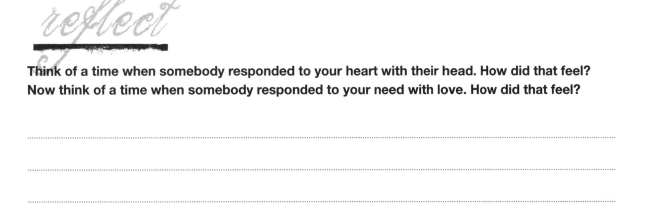

Think of a time when somebody responded to your heart with their head. How did that feel? Now think of a time when somebody responded to your need with love. How did that feel?

....

....

....

....

THE "I" MESSAGE

Effective Communication

"I" Messages

"I feel ... "

"When ..."

"I need to feel ..."

For Example:

"I feel scared when you drive like this. I need to feel safe and protected while I am in the car with you."

"It hurts me when you talk to me like this. I need to hear about you and feel valued while we talk."

"I love it when we are together. I need to feel like this more often."

An "I" message is a tool that lets you see me instead of trying to convince you that you are wrong.

- An "I" message is fueled by a feeling, not a thought. If you can put the word "think" in a sentence and it makes sense, it's not a feeling.

- Feelings tell you about me, not about you. For example, "I feel hurt. I feel rejected. When this happened, I felt sad," not "I feel like you are a jerk. I feel like you are evil."

- It's important to handle the toxic emotions of fear and hurt carefully.

Protecting our connection is more important than my need to be right or to do what I want.

- When I share my feelings with you, there's an into-me-you-see moment, and you get to respond to my heart.

reflect

On your own, brainstorm some "I" messages that will accurately portray what you often feel in your relationship without pointing the finger at your significant other.

Discuss these questions together as a class or in small groups.

1. Why do you think communication is one of the most common problems in marriage?

2. What is your communication style: passive, aggressive, passive-aggressive, assertive? Give examples.

3. How would you define intimacy?

Take some time to communicate as a couple, either after class or during the week.

1. Has understanding or agreement been your goal in communication?

2. What communication styles have you been using and how has that affected your relationship?

3. Have you been able to experience the euphoria of vulnerable intimacy together (without sex)?

4. Do you feel safe sharing the truth with each other, or are there still walls of fear in place? (The walls may not have originated from this relationship.)

1. **On your own** go back through the session notes and write out your answers to the *Reflect* questions.

2. **Together** discuss the *Communicate* questions and talk through any issues or topics that were brought up during the session.

3. **Journal** your thoughts and dreams as you walk through the journey of this course.

journal

Conflict
MANAGEMENT

8

Conflict MANAGEMENT 8

session eight

HAVING A PLAN
I NEED, I NEED!
PROTECTING THE CONNECTION

HAVING A PLAN

Having a plan for how to resolve conflict will help you maneuver through the difficult parts of your relationships.

- You need to have a plan for what you're going to do, no matter what the other person does.

- Resolving conflict has everything to do with a process.

- You get to decide how many disrespectful interactions you're going to participate in. That is your responsibility and choice.

- The other person in conflict doesn't need to be a great communicator for you to handle the situation well. You just have to know when you're going to stop participating in the exchange.

"Think of a sixty-inch flat screen TV and a Blu-ray player. In order to display a message, you need both a speaker and a listener. There's no way of knowing what the coded message on a disc is until it is placed in that processor, and then the processor sends that information across the line and the TV displays that information on the screen. The TV doesn't judge the disc, saying, 'Oh, that's a stupid movie. I've seen it!' Instead it says, 'Is this what you're saying? Is this what you're trying to tell me? Is this accurate?' Like the TV, the listener's job is so important because otherwise, the message isn't heard. And, like the Blu-ray, the speaker's job is to send the message with as much clarity as possible. Both are necessary. Classically, there are two Blue-ray players both trying to display a message, but there is no listener! Just somebody talking like crazy!"

COMMUNICATION PROCESS

flat screen tv

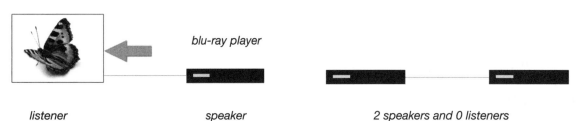

blu-ray player

listener   *speaker*

THE GREAT COMMUNICATION PERIL

2 speakers and 0 listeners

reflect

In your relationships, are you most often the speaker or the listener? What does most of your communication look like?

....

....

....

....

I NEED, I NEED!

Unresolved need is one of the greatest issues in relational conflict.

- When needs go unmet, the belief that you care about me is in doubt.

- The listener is the winner during a conflict, because they now have two pieces of information: I know what you need, and I know what I need.

- People need to know that they have a safe place to communicate what they need. This feels like love.

- In order to find a solution, you need to communicate what the problem is. You need to communicate what it is that you need.

- Communicate your needs without pointing a finger at the other person.

**Trust is developed
when needs are expressed**

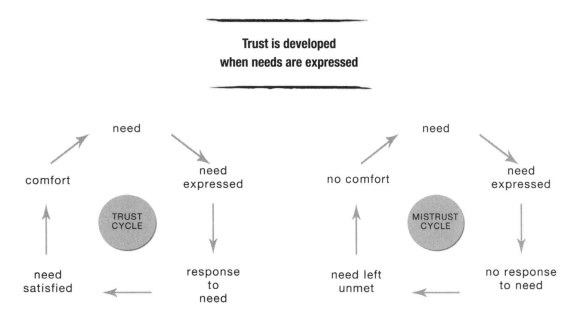

Getting my needs met just requires showing you my heart, and then you can respond.

- When communicating needs, few words are better than many.

- Proverbs 10:19 *"When there are many words, transgression is unavoidable, but he who restrains his lips is wise."*

- Communicate your needs, and then allow your significant other to decide how to meet those needs.

- Ultimately, you take responsibility for your half of the relationship. I'll take responsibility for mine.

- If you don't communicate what you need, you won't get your needs met.

- Communicate needs without using anxiety and manipulation. When I come to serve you, you feel exalted. When you turn me into a servant, I feel humiliated.

reflect

What needs do you have in your relationship? What needs have you noticed that your significant other has? How have you discovered those?

....

....

....

....

....

....

....

Our connection with each other is way more important than any conflict, and our need to connect is deeper than our need to be right!

Skyler & Kim

PROTECTING THE CONNECTION

By listening to your significant other and trying to discover their needs, you are inviting the best part of them into the conflict instead of the worst.

- Discovering a person's needs will often enable you to disarm their anxiety, because they will feel understood.

- Many people struggle with conflict because they decide that if you don't care about them, they are not going to care about you, but that is allowing someone else to be in charge of your character and behavior.

- You find out how strong your internal world really is when people are being scary and hurtful.

If you don't bring your love to a conflict, the worst part of you will be on display.

- Speak and listen using the "I" message until the anxiety drops.

- Galatians 6:1 (NIV) *"Brothers, if someone is caught in a sin, you who are spiritual should restore him gently."*

- Coming to a conflict in a spirit of gentleness says, "I don't need control of you. I've come to you to tell you what's going on inside of me."

Here's the basics of conflict resolution:
I've come to you about me.
I want to hear about you.

Disconnection happens when conflict remains unresolved.

- In many families, it is normal to have unstable connections.

- Once a couple has a momentum for protecting their relationship, it becomes easier to resolve conflict and retain their connection.

- When in a disconnect, remember their love language and the "I" message.

- Remind yourself of who is in charge of you. Manage yourself towards your goal of connection.

The better you get at resolving conflict,
the more your relationship becomes about
managing *how* connected you are,
not *if* you're connected.

---

reflect

Can you think of a time when you pointed out someone else's problem instead of expressing your need? How did it go? How about a time when you chose to show your heart and be vulnerable? How did that go?

....

....

....

....

....

....

....

....

....

....

....

....

....

....

Discuss these questions together as a class or in small groups.

1. Is conflict a bad thing? Why?

2. What would a healthy conflict resolution plan look like?

3. When communicating your needs, why do you think it is better to have few words rather than many?

4. Discuss some practical ways to build up connection again after a disconnect.

Take some time to communicate as a couple, either after class or during the week.

1. What are some needs that have gone un-met in your lives? How did that feel and what did you do about it?

2. What would it look like for both of you to take responsibility for your half of the relationship only? Has that been evident in your relationship?

3. Have you been in conflict together before? If so, did the worst or best part of you show up in the conversation? Explain.

4. How have you experienced connection? Is it unstable? Or are you usually connected with slight disconnects from time to time?

1. **On your own** go back through the session notes and write out your answers to the *Reflect* questions.

2. **Together** discuss the *Communicate* questions and talk through any issues or topics that were brought up during the session.

3. **Journal** your thoughts and dreams as you walk through the journey of this course.

journal

The 90/10
FACTOR

9

The 90/10 FACTOR

9

session nine

INTIMACY "IN-TO-ME-SEE"
BUILDING THE STRENGTH OF OUR CONNECTION
A 90/10 CYCLE

INTIMACY "IN-TO-ME-SEE"

The goal of relationship is intimacy experienced through connection.

- The building of intimate connections is rooted in truth and trust.

- Marriage is a process of blending two lives together, like cementing or gluing together two boards.

For this reason a man shall leave his father and his mother,
and be joined to his wife; and they shall become one flesh.

Genesis 2:24 (NASB)

- Broken covenants, such as divorce, are so devastating because what was joined together as one is now ripped apart. Part of you is stuck on me, and part of me is stuck on you.

If you're going to create a covenant with someone, you have to bring your whole self to the table.

- Inner healing is about rebuilding and restoring your ability to make covenants and to experience intimacy.

- If you can't bring your whole heart to a relationship, intimacy will be very difficult for you, because you will constantly be on your guard.

Intimacy has to happen with the Perfect One before it will ever happen with an imperfect one.

Webster's definition: *in·ti·ma·cy* (n)
1. a close personal relationship
2. a quiet and private atmosphere
3. a detailed knowledge resulting from a close or long association or study
4. a private and personal utterance or action
5. a sexual act or sexual intercourse (used euphemistically)

Intimacy says, "You can be you around me. I want to know you. I value you."

- "In-to-me-see"

    See the real me

    Know the real me

    Accept the real me

    - *Can I be real with you?*

    - *Can you handle who I am?*

    - *Will you value who I am?*

    - *Will you still love me, as I am?*

- If intimacy is not our goal, our experience together will fall short of what was intended for relationships.

- The practice of communication and building connection must be purposeful.

- The more I mature in my relationships, the more aware I become of how my behavior affects other people.

reflect

Are you experiencing intimacy as described above?

....

....

....

BUILDING THE STRENGTH OF OUR CONNECTION

The strength of your connection is revealed when the relationship is tested.

John 6:56 *"Whoever eats my flesh and drinks my blood remains in me, and I in him."*

What was Jesus thinking? Was He in a strange mood? Having a bad day? No, Jesus was testing the strength of connections. Because this was a statement that would require people to search deeper, many people who had fragile relationships with Him were shaken off. But who stood by Him? His disciples. They weren't going to let go. They had nowhere else to go, and Jesus had all the life they needed. Jesus knew that one day they would be required to give even their lives for Him, yet they would still hang onto their end of the relationship. To what end are you willing to hang onto your relationships?

The practice of intimacy is this: *I will not let go.*

- We will see the strength of our relationship the moment we have two strong opposing views.

- When you have the *La La La* factor, you are not expressing your strong opposing views; you are expressing only the ones you agree on.

reflect

Has your relationship been tested? How? What was the strength of it?

....

....

....

A 90/10 CYCLE

Men and women are comprised of very different needs and motivations.

- Men have testosterone pumping through their veins and were designed that way on purpose. It's not evil!

- The hope of sexual behavior motivates them to direct their attentions to a woman.

- Women are motivated by the hope of a heart-to-heart connection with your man. Emotions direct much of their behaviors towards him. They were designed this way on purpose.

- Neither the man's nor the woman's needs and desires are wrong; they are simply different.

In order to build connection with your significant other, you have to understand and value their needs.

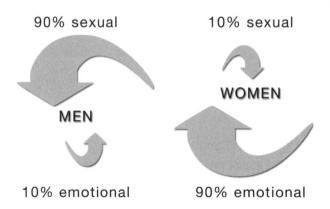

90% sexual   10% sexual

MEN   WOMEN

10% emotional   90% emotional

- Primarily, men are 90% sexually motivated and 10% emotionally motivated.

- Women are usually 90% emotionally motivated and 10% sexually motivated.

- Paying attention to this cycle ensures both sets of needs are met.

- It is important for women to establish a non-sexual soul tie with their man before being married so that he knows and practices meeting those needs beforehand.

- A man must learn to serve a woman's emotions and love her as Christ loves the Church, sacrificing Himself for her.

- Feelings and needs are emotional experiences. As men meet the needs in their women, she will feel safe, loved, and able to be vulnerable with you.

**Sex is about intimacy,
being both physically and emotionally
vulnerable with each other.**

Using other means to satisfy your needs will demotivate you to pursue your mate.

- It is expensive for men to introduce sexual behaviors outside of their relationship with their wife. It demotivates the man to pursue her needs.

- If women allow other men or other emotional experiences to satisfy their emotional needs, it demotivates them to pursue his needs.

- One of the biggest areas of conflict in marriage is this: I don't feel valued or loved. Breakdown in marriage happens when this cycle is not understood.

Saving yourself both physically and emotionally will make your marriage awesome!

Skyler & Kim

Understanding your spouse's love languages will help you to fulfill their emotional and sexual needs.

- Communication of your needs is paramount; your spouse can't read your mind!

- Remember that nobody can manage your love, honor, truth, responsibility, vision, and faith but you.

reflect

How well have you been communicating your needs to your significant other? If you have not been communicating them, what is keeping you from doing so?

....

....

....

....

....

....

....

....

....

....

....

....

....

....

Discuss these questions together as a class or in small groups.

1. How has this teaching affected your view of the opposite sex?

2. If you come from a broken background, how can you bring your whole heart to a new relationship?

3. Why is it so important to have a healthy relationship with the Father before pursuing a significant relationship with someone else?

4. Do you find the 90/10 Factor to be true in your relationship?

Take some time to communicate as a couple, either after class or during the week.

1. What is the goal for your relationship?

2. How is your connection? How is your understanding?

3. In what ways have you seen your relationship tested? Have these experiences helped you to grow as a couple?

4. Discuss your views on pre-marital purity. What boundaries have you established to protect your marriage?

1. **On your own** go back through the session notes and write out your answers to the *Reflect* questions.

2. **Together** discuss the *Communicate* questions and talk through any issues or topics that were brought up during the session.

3. **Journal** your thoughts and dreams as you walk through the journey of this course.

journal

references

**The Five Love Languages: How to Express Heartfelt Commitment
To Your Mate**
by Gary Chapman   Chicago, IL: Northfield Publishing (1992, 1995, 2004, 2010)

The Path: Creating Your Mission Statement For Work And For Life
by Jones, L.B.   New York: Hyperion (1996)

resources

Loving On Purpose
ministry of Danny & Sheri Silk   www.LovingOnPurpose.com

Other Relational Resources from Loving On Purpose:

Becoming a Man
Community of Believers
Insert Love Here
Keys to Confrontation
Loving Our Kids on Purpose
Men and Women
Process of Love
Who's Our Daddy

Prepare/Enrich Assessment
www.Prepare-Enrich.com

Financial Keys For Couples
cd/dvd by Steve De Silva   www.ProsperousSoul.com